KOBE BRYANT: A BOOK FOR SMART KIDS

From Philly to LA: The Journey of a Legend and the Making of an NBA Superstar

---

MAGIC MATTHEWS

Life is too short to get bogged down and be discouraged. You have to keep moving. You have to keep going. Put one foot in front of the other, smile, and just keep on rolling.

- Kobe Bryant

Contents

Introduction

Kobe Bryant is a name that stands tall in the world of sports. But his story isn't just about basketball — it's about hard work, determination, and the unwavering belief that you can achieve greatness no matter where you start. Born in Philadelphia in 1978, Kobe grew up around basketball. His father, Joe "Jellybean" Bryant, was a professional player, and from a young age, Kobe knew that he wanted to follow in his dad's footsteps.

What set Kobe apart was his incredible drive and dedication. Even as a kid, he practiced for hours, determined to be the best. *Kobe Bryant: A Book for Smart Kids - From Philly to LA:The Journey of a Legend and the Making of an NBA Superstar*, tells the inspiring story of how Kobe went from being a young boy with big dreams to one of the greatest basketball players of all time.

Kobe's journey wasn't easy. He faced challenges, injuries, and setbacks, but he never gave up. He worked harder, pushed himself further, and believed that anything was possible if he put in the effort. Along the way, he won five NBA championships, earned the nickname "The Black

Mamba," and showed the world what true greatness looks like.

This book explores Kobe's incredible career — from his early years growing up in Italy and Philadelphia, to his time with the Los Angeles Lakers, and beyond. It's a story of resilience, passion, and a mindset that focuses on constant improvement, hard work, and overcoming obstacles.

Kobe's legacy isn't just about basketball; it's about inspiring others to dream big, work hard, and believe in themselves. Whether you're a basketball fan or just looking for a story about someone who never gave up, Kobe's journey will show you that with determination and heart, anything is possible.

Let's dive into the life of a true legend — Kobe Bryant.

ONE

Early Years: Growing Up in Philadelphia

Kobe Bryant was born on August 23, 1978, in Philadelphia, Pennsylvania. His parents, Joe and Pamela Bryant, gave him a unique name after seeing "Kobe" on a menu in a Japanese restaurant, referring to a special kind of beef from Japan. From the very beginning, his parents had a feeling their son would be extraordinary, and they weren't wrong. Kobe was the youngest of three children, with two older sisters, Sharia who was five years older than Kobe and Shaya, who was three years older than him.

Growing up, Kobe was surrounded by basketball. His father, Joe Bryant, was a professional basketball player in the NBA (National Basketball Association). The NBA is the top professional basketball league in the United States, where the best basketball players in the world compete. With Joe playing in the league, basketball was always present in their home, and Kobe grew up watching, learning, and falling in love with the game. Joe's career took the family to various places and allowed Kobe to be immersed in the basketball world from a young age.

Kobe's mother, Pamela, played a crucial role in keeping the family grounded. Though she wasn't an athlete like her husband, Pamela worked hard to support her family, both emotionally and practically. She took on the role of caregiver, making sure the Bryant household ran smoothly as they navigated Joe's career and frequent relocations.

Kobe always spoke fondly of how his mother, Pamela, created a warm and supportive environment at home. She was the glue that held the family together during their frequent relocations due to Joe Bryant's basketball career. Kobe once mentioned that his mother was the one who encouraged him to be disciplined not only in sports but in life, teaching him the importance of balance and family values.

By the time Kobe was three years old, he had already developed a love for the game. He would watch his dad play basketball on TV and try to imitate him. Using a mini trampoline and a plastic hoop, Kobe would launch himself into the air to dunk a ball, pretending he was playing in the NBA just like his dad. It was clear, even at such a young age, that basketball was going to be a big part of Kobe's life.

When Kobe was six, a big change happened in his family's life. Joe Bryant, his father, decided to continue his basketball career overseas and moved the entire family to Italy. Kobe's dad had already spent eight seasons in the NBA, and now he wanted to try playing basketball in Europe. The Bryant family settled in a small town called Rieti, about fifty miles (approximately 80.47 kilometers) from Rome. It was a completely new world for Kobe and his sisters. They didn't speak any Italian at first, and everything around them felt unfamiliar.

But Kobe, being the determined kid he was, quickly adapted. He spent time with his sisters, Sharia and Shaya, helping each other learn Italian. Before long, Kobe was speaking Italian fluently, making friends, and adjusting to life in his new home. Italy would become a place of fond memories for Kobe, a place where he began to shape his future as a basketball player.

In Italy, Kobe's love for basketball continued to grow. His father played for different teams across the country, and wherever the family moved, there was always a basketball court nearby. Kobe would often practice with his father's team and even joined the youth squad of the teams Joe played for. Although he was much younger than the other players, his basketball skills were already beginning to shine.

Kobe's mom, Pamela, was a strong influence in his life, especially when it came to discipline and focus. She had a serious approach to life, and Kobe seemed to inherit that same seriousness when it came to basketball. His sister Sharia once said that Kobe was always intensely focused, even when he was just a kid. He hardly ever smiled when he played, but you could tell he loved the game. He was determined to be the best.

While living in Italy, Kobe also developed a love for soccer. In fact, soccer was one of his favorite sports growing up. He became a fan of A.C. Milan, a famous Italian soccer team. But even though soccer was fun for him, basketball was always number one. Every summer, Kobe and his family would travel back to the United States, where he would take advantage of the opportunity to sharpen his basketball skills. During these trips, Kobe joined competitive basketball leagues, facing off against other talented young players. These summer leagues were intense and filled with strong competition, giving Kobe the chance to test his abilities against some of the best players his age. He spent hours on the court, practicing and working to improve his shooting, dribbling, and footwork.

Even though Kobe was far away from the NBA, his grandfather, Grandpa Cox, made sure he didn't miss out on the action. Grandpa Cox would record NBA games on VHS tapes, box them up, and send them all the way to Italy. Kobe would watch those games over and over again, studying every move made by the NBA stars. His favorite player was Michael Jordan, and Kobe dreamed of one day playing in the NBA, just like his hero.

Kobe's father, Joe, continued to play for various teams in Italy, which meant the family moved around a lot. They lived in several cities, including Reggio Calabria, Pistoia, and Reggio Emilia. Within this time, Kobe and his sisters received their education through a combination of local schools and private tutoring, allowing them to adapt to the constant moves. Despite the challenges of relocating, Kobe's parents made sure that academics were prioritized. Each place brought new adventures for Kobe, but no matter where they went, basketball was always a constant part of his life. In fact, during his time in Italy, Kobe even served as a ball boy for his father's team. A ball boy is a person, usually someone young, who assists during games by retrieving balls that go out of play, handing players towels, and making sure the court stays clean and dry. Kobe's job as a ball boy allowed him to be right in the middle of the action, observing professional players up close and learning from them. At halftime, Kobe would shoot hoops on the court, impressing everyone with his talent. One of Joe's former teammates, Leon Douglas, remembered how Kobe would take over the court at halftime, showing off his shooting skills. It was clear to everyone that Kobe was something special.

As much as Kobe loved Italy, another big change came when he was thirteen years old. In 1991, the Bryant family decided to return to the United States, settling back in Philadelphia, after spending a total of seven years in Italy. For Kobe, this was both exciting and challenging. Although he had been born in Philadelphia, moving back felt strange. He didn't understand the slang kids were using, and he wasn't familiar with American culture. Even though he spoke English fluently, having spent much of his childhood in Italy made him feel different from his peers.

Despite these initial challenges, Kobe soon realized that his return to America was the beginning of a new chapter, one filled with endless opportunities to prove himself and rise to greatness.

TWO

High School Stardom: Lower Merion's Rising Star

When Kobe Bryant returned to the United States in 1991, his life was about to change in ways he couldn't have imagined. After living in Italy for years, where he'd developed his love for basketball, Kobe found himself in Philadelphia once again. It wasn't easy at first — he had to adjust to a new culture, new friends, and a new way of life. But one thing remained constant: his passion for basketball. He enrolled in Bala Cynwyd Middle School for eighth grade and quickly found his rhythm both in school and on the basketball court.

After middle school, Kobe moved on to Lower Merion High School in Ardmore, a suburb of Philadelphia. Lower Merion was where Kobe's talent would shine and where he would make a name for himself as one of the best young basketball players in the country. At just fourteen years old, Kobe did something almost unheard of — he made the varsity basketball team as a freshman. The varsity team is the main sports team representing a high school or college in competitions, usually made up of the best and most experienced players. It's rare for freshmen, who are often younger and less experienced, to play on a varsity team, as most spots are filled by upperclassmen. But Kobe's talent and skills were so advanced that he earned his place among the older, more experienced players.

That first year was tough though. The Lower Merion Aces, the school's basketball team, struggled during Kobe's freshman season, ending with a disappointing 4-20 record.

This means that out of the twenty-four games they played that season, they won only four and lost twenty. In basketball, each game you win adds a point to your win column, and each game you lose adds a point to your loss column. The goal is to win as many games as possible during the season to have a strong record, and ideally, a winning team will have more wins than losses.

Even though the team didn't win many games, Kobe's potential was obvious to everyone who watched him play. He was only fourteen years old and already playing against older, stronger players, which was an incredible accomplishment on its own. But Kobe wasn't discouraged by the tough season or the team's struggles. Instead, he used the experience as fuel to get better. He practiced even harder, determined to improve both his skills and his understanding of the game. Kobe didn't just want to improve for himself; he wanted to help his team succeed. His mindset was always about growth, and he believed that hard work would eventually lead to better results.

Kobe spent countless hours practicing. He wasn't the type of player to rely on talent alone. He knew that hard work was what separated good players from great players. Whether it was early mornings, late evenings, or weekends, you could almost always find Kobe in the gym, perfecting his shot, improving his footwork, and working on his defense. His work ethic was unmatched, and it wasn't long before all that hard work began to pay off.

By his sophomore (second) year of high school, things started to change. Kobe had gained more experience and confidence, and the team began winning games. Over the next three years, Kobe's presence on the team completely transformed the Lower Merion Aces. From that point on, they became a powerhouse, and Kobe was the driving force behind their success.

During his time on the team, Kobe played all five positions — point guard, shooting guard, small forward, power forward, and even center. Each of these positions has a specific role, and it's rare for a player to be able to play them all, but Kobe was able to do it with ease. The point guard is like the leader on the court, responsible for running plays and setting up the offense. The shooting guard is usually the best shooter on the team, focused on scoring points from outside shots and driving to the basket. The small forward is versatile, able to shoot, dribble, and defend, often switching between playing inside and outside the three-point line. The power forward is strong and tough, playing near the basket to grab rebounds and score from close range, while the center, usually the tallest player, defends the basket, blocks shots, and scores from underneath. Kobe's ability to play all these positions showed just how skilled and versatile he was, making him unstoppable on the court and a huge advantage for his team.

In his junior year, at the age of sixteen years old, Kobe's performance skyrocketed. Kobe's stats during this year were incredible. He averaged 31.1 points per game, which means in each game, he scored over thirty-one points by making baskets. In basketball, a player can score one, two, or three points depending on the type of shot they make. For example, free throws are worth one point, regular shots made inside the three-point line are worth two points, and shots made beyond the three-point line are worth three points.

Kobe also averaged 10.4 rebounds per game. A rebound happens when a player grabs the ball after a missed shot, either on offense (trying to score again) or defense (stopping the other team from getting another chance to score). Grabbing over ten rebounds per game showed how strong and active Kobe was around the basket.

With 5.2 assists per game, Kobe helped his teammates score by passing the ball to them at the right time. An assist is when a player passes the ball to a teammate, and that teammate scores right after receiving the pass. It's a sign of a good team player who knows how to set up others to score.

He also averaged 3.8 blocks per game, meaning he stopped nearly four shots each game by blocking them before they could reach the basket. Blocking shots is a key defensive skill, especially when playing against strong offensive players.

Lastly, Kobe averaged 2.3 steals per game, which means he took the ball away from the opposing team while they were trying to pass or dribble. A steal helps stop the other team from scoring and can often lead to a quick basket for your team.

These impressive stats showed that Kobe wasn't just a great scorer; he did everything on the court — scoring, defending, passing, and helping his team win in every way possible.

His dominance was clear, and people were starting to take notice. Kobe's exceptional play earned him the title of Pennsylvania Player of the Year, a prestigious honor recognizing the best high school basketball player in the state. He also earned a Parade All-American nomination, which was given to the best high school players in the country. It wasn't just local coaches and fans who noticed how talented Kobe was — college scouts were coming to watch him play. Schools like Duke, Michigan, North Carolina, and Villanova really wanted him to join their basketball teams.

As Kobe's junior year came to an end, something else caught his attention: the NBA. In 1995, a high school player named Kevin Garnett was selected directly into the NBA, skipping college altogether. This opened Kobe's eyes to the possibility of doing the same. He began to think seriously about going straight to the pros instead of attending college. After all, he was already practicing with NBA players during the summers.

During the Adidas ABCD Camp, a famous basketball camp where the best high school players in the country came to compete, Kobe truly shined. He played alongside future NBA stars like Lamar Odom and earned the camp's MVP (most valuable player) award. His skills were on full display, and it became clear to everyone that Kobe was destined for greatness. Even John Lucas, the coach of the Philadelphia 76ers at the time, invited Kobe to work out and practice with the team. Kobe, still in high school, got the chance to play one-on-one with Jerry Stackhouse, one of the NBA's top players. This experience further fueled Kobe's desire to skip college and head straight to the NBA.

Kobe's senior year at Lower Merion was nothing short of spectacular. By now, he was a national sensation, with everyone in the basketball world talking about him. During his final season with the Aces, Kobe led the team to a 31-3 record, winning the Pennsylvania state championship. It was the school's first state title in fifty-three years, and Kobe was the star of the show. He averaged 30.8 points, twelve rebounds, 6.5 assists, four steals, and 3.8 blocks per game. His ability to do everything on the court — score, defend, rebound, and pass — made him one of the most complete high school players anyone had ever seen.

Kobe's performance that year didn't just lead to a state championship; it also earned him numerous individual awards. He was named the Naismith High School Player of the Year, which recognized him as the best high school player in the entire country. He also received the Gatorade Men's National Basketball Player of the Year Award, a McDonald's All-American honor, and a spot on the USA Today All-USA First Team. These were some of the most prestigious awards a high school basketball player could earn, and Kobe had earned them all.

Kobe's high school coach, Greg Downer, often spoke about Kobe's unmatched work ethic and drive. Downer once said, "Kobe was a complete player who dominated every aspect of the game. He wasn't just the best player on the team; he was the hardest worker too." Even though Kobe was clearly the most talented player, he never took his success for granted. He worked harder than anyone else, and that's what made him stand out.

During his senior year, Kobe made headlines off the court when he took R&B singer Brandy to his prom. Brandy was already a famous singer and actress, and Kobe was quickly becoming well-known in the basketball world. Everyone was talking about it because it was a big deal for a high school student to go to prom with such a popular celebrity. It was clear that Kobe wasn't just any regular student — he was on his way to becoming a superstar!

With all of his achievements in high school, Kobe had many options for his future. He had received scholarship offers from nearly every top college basketball program in the country, but he knew in his heart that college wasn't for him. Kobe wanted to go straight to the NBA. At just seventeen years old, Kobe made the bold decision to skip college and declare for the NBA Draft, following in the footsteps of Kevin Garnett. It was a decision that shocked many, but Kobe was confident in his abilities.

On April 29, 1996, Kobe held a press conference at his high school gym, surrounded by teammates, coaches, family, and reporters. With the cameras rolling, Kobe made his announcement: "I've decided to skip college and take my talent to the NBA." The crowd erupted in cheers, and Kobe flashed his signature smile. He was only the sixth player in history to make the jump from high school directly to the NBA, but Kobe knew he was ready.

By the time he finished high school, Kobe Bryant had become the all-time leading scorer in Southeastern Pennsylvania history, finishing with 2,883 points. He had surpassed legends like Wilt Chamberlain and Lionel Simmons, cementing his place as one of the greatest high school players ever.

Kobe's high school journey was nothing short of remarkable. From starting on the varsity team as a freshman to becoming a national sensation by his senior year, Kobe had proven that hard work, dedication, and an unrelenting desire to be the best could take him to unimaginable heights. And while his time at Lower Merion had come to an end, his journey was just beginning. The NBA awaited, and Kobe Bryant was ready to take on the world.

THREE

Lakers Rookie: A Star in the Making

Going straight to the NBA after high school was a really
bold move because only a few players had ever done it
before. Everyone was excited to see what Kobe could do,
but first, he had to prove himself. So, before the NBA draft,
Kobe had the chance to play against some former Lakers
stars like Larry Drew and Michael Cooper. Kobe didn't
just compete with them — he dominated! The Lakers'

general manager, Jerry West, said that Kobe completely outplayed them, showing that he was more than ready for the big league.

The Lakers really wanted Kobe on their team, but to make it happen, they had to make some big changes. They were hoping to sign one of the biggest basketball stars at the time, Shaquille O'Neal, who was a powerful player and one of the best in the league. But to bring Shaq to the Lakers, they needed to free up some money to pay him. To do this, they had to trade one of their current players, Vlade Divac, and get a better spot in the NBA Draft to choose a young player like Kobe.

The NBA Draft system plays a crucial role in this process. Each year, teams in the league get to select new players, often young prospects coming out of college or high school, based on their draft position. The teams with the worst records are entered into a lottery for the top picks, giving them a higher chance to select top talent and rebuild. This system is designed to maintain competitive balance across the league. The better a team did in the previous season, the later they get to pick in the draft.

The Charlotte Hornets, another team in the NBA, had the 13th pick in the draft, which meant they could choose one of the top players that year. The Lakers made a deal with the Hornets: the Hornets would pick Kobe with their 13th pick, and then they would trade him to the Lakers. But the catch was that the Hornets had to trust the Lakers to tell them which player to pick. So, during the 1996 NBA Draft, the Hornets selected Kobe Bryant, and right after, they traded him to the Lakers.

Since Kobe was only seventeen years old when all of this happened, he was still too young to sign his own contract, which is the agreement between a player and a team about how long they'll play and how much they'll get paid. Because of his age, Kobe's parents had to sign his first contract for him. His first deal was for three years and worth $3.5 million — a lot of money for someone who had just graduated from high school! It was an exciting moment for Kobe, but he knew the real work was just beginning. Now, he had to prove he could compete with the best players in the world.

As soon as Kobe joined the Lakers, everyone was buzzing with excitement. His first taste of the NBA came in the Summer Pro League in Long Beach, California. This league was designed to give new players a chance to show what they could do. In his very first game, Kobe scored twenty-five points, and the crowd went wild. His speed and moves made it hard for defenders to keep up, and by the time the league ended, Kobe had impressed everyone by averaging 24.5 points and 5.3 rebounds in just four games.

When the real NBA season started, Kobe was one of the youngest players ever to play in an NBA game — he was just eighteen years and seventy-two days old! That's super young to be playing with pros who had been in the league for years. Even though he had incredible talent, Kobe had to be patient. The Lakers already had some experienced players like Eddie Jones and Nick Van Exel, so Kobe mostly came off the bench in his first season, only playing a few minutes each game. But Kobe wasn't discouraged — he kept practicing hard and learning from the older players.

As the season went on, Kobe started to get more playing time. By the end of his first year, he was averaging 15.5 minutes per game, which was quite remarkable for an eighteen year old straight out of high school. Most high school draftees rarely see significant time on the court in their first year, so Kobe's ability to earn those minutes highlighted his potential and dedication.

During the All-Star weekend, one of the most exciting events of the NBA season, Kobe took part in the Slam Dunk Contest. This is a fun and thrilling competition where players show off their most creative and high-flying dunks. A dunk is when a player jumps and slams the ball into the basket with their hands, often with lots of power and style. The goal is to impress the judges and the crowd with how amazing the dunk looks.

Kobe didn't just participate — he stole the show. His dunks were so incredible and full of style that the judges and fans were blown away. Kobe made difficult dunks look easy, jumping high and throwing the ball into the basket with flair. His performance was so impressive that he ended up winning the contest! At just eighteen years old, he became the youngest player ever to win the Slam Dunk Contest, which was a huge achievement.

This victory got everyone talking about Kobe, and it wasn't just because of his dunks. Winning the Slam Dunk Contest showed that Kobe wasn't afraid of the big stage and could handle the pressure of performing in front of a huge audience. It also boosted his confidence, making him believe even more in his abilities and showing that he was ready for bigger challenges in the NBA.

The Lakers made it to the playoffs that year, which is a special tournament where the best teams in the NBA compete for the championship. During Game Five against the Utah Jazz, the Lakers found themselves in a tough spot. Some of the team's key players, like Byron Scott and Robert Horry, were unable to play due to injuries and foul trouble, which meant that Kobe, who was still young, had to take on a bigger role. This was a big deal for Kobe because the game was very important, and a lot was at stake.

Kobe tried his best to help the team, but he missed some important shots — four in total, including three shots from beyond the three-point line during overtime (the extra time played when the game is tied at the end of regular time). The Lakers ended up losing the game. Missing those shots could have made him feel bad, but instead of getting discouraged, Kobe chose to learn from it.

Even Shaquille O'Neal, one of the biggest stars on the team, had something positive to say about Kobe. Shaq pointed out that even though Kobe missed the shots, he was the only player brave enough to take them in such a high-pressure situation.

In his second year, Kobe really started to shine. He got more playing time and began showing everyone what he could do. His points per game more than doubled, going from 7.6 points in his first season to 15.4 points in his second season. The Lakers also sometimes played a style of basketball called "playing small." This meant that instead of using bigger players for certain positions, they used quicker, more athletic players like Kobe. This allowed Kobe to play as a small forward, a position that gave him more chances to show what he could do on the court, like scoring, passing, and defending. It was a great opportunity for him to use his full range of skills and help his team.

He was also voted to play in the NBA All-Star Game, and not just as a regular player — Kobe became the youngest starter in All-Star history at only nineteen years old! That was a huge accomplishment, and it proved that Kobe was on his way to becoming a superstar.

By his third season, Kobe was starting to make a name for himself as one of the best young guards in the league. With Nick Van Exel and Eddie Jones traded to other teams, Kobe became a full-time starter for the Lakers. Even though the season was shortened due to a lockout, Kobe made every game count. During that season, he also signed a six-year contract worth seventy million dollars, securing his future with the Lakers for years to come.

People were starting to compare Kobe to NBA legends like Michael Jordan and Magic Johnson. His scoring ability, his footwork, and his incredible work ethic made everyone realize that Kobe was something special. Although the Lakers were eliminated in the playoffs by the San Antonio Spurs, Kobe's future was looking brighter than ever.

In just a few short years, Kobe had gone from a high school kid with big dreams to one of the most exciting young players in the NBA. He had faced challenges along the way, like missing those shots in the playoffs, but each time, Kobe used those experiences to get better. With his talent, determination, and love for the game, Kobe was just getting started, and the world was beginning to see that he was destined to be one of the greatest basketball players ever.

FOUR

Championship Dreams: Teaming Up with Shaq

By the time Kobe Bryant reached his fourth season in the NBA in 1999, he was becoming one of the league's biggest stars. But what made this season even more special was that the Lakers got a new coach named Phil Jackson. Phil Jackson was already a legendary coach because he had helped Michael Jordan and the Chicago Bulls win six NBA championships. Now, he was in Los

Angeles to lead the Lakers, and he had a plan to make the most of Kobe Bryant's and Shaquille O'Neal's talents.

Kobe and Shaq were an incredible combination on the court. Kobe was an amazing scorer who could shoot from the outside, and he was known for his fast moves and his ability to drive straight to the basket. His dunks were so acrobatic that they looked like something out of an Olympic gymnastics routine. Meanwhile, Shaq was a force of nature. He was over seven feet tall (over 213.36 centimeters) and weighed more than 300 pounds (136 kilograms), so when he dunked, it was nearly impossible to stop him. His dunks were so powerful that they shook the backboard. Together, Kobe and Shaq made a great team, with Kobe's speed and skill matching Shaq's incredible strength.

With Phil Jackson's coaching and his famous triangle offense, the Lakers became an unstoppable team. The triangle offense was a strategy that allowed both Kobe and Shaq to play to their strengths, making it easier for them to dominate games. It also helped them work together, even though they had different styles of playing.

In the 1999–2000 season, Kobe had a bit of a setback early on. During a preseason game against the Washington Wizards, Kobe injured his hand when he collided with another player. He ended up breaking a bone in his right hand, which was a tough blow. As a result, he had to sit out for six weeks to heal properly. Missing that time was hard for Kobe, who always wanted to be on the court helping his team.

But Kobe didn't waste time while he was recovering. Even though he couldn't play, he stayed focused on studying the game and keeping his body in shape. He used this time to improve his mental approach, learning more about basketball strategies and how he could make an even bigger impact once he was back. When he finally returned to the court, he was better than ever, showing everyone how determined and dedicated he was.

He led the team in assists and steals, showing how much he had improved in every area. That season, the Lakers won sixty-seven games, one of the best records in NBA history. Shaq was named the NBA's Most Valuable Player (MVP), and Kobe was recognized on both the All-NBA Second Team and the All-Defensive Team for the first time in his career.

The Lakers fought through the playoffs, with Kobe playing a huge role in their success. One of his most memorable moments came in Game Seven of the Western Conference Finals against the Portland Trail Blazers. Kobe had a spectacular game, scoring twenty-five points, grabbing eleven rebounds, and making seven assists. He even threw a game-changing pass to Shaq that helped the Lakers win and move on to the NBA Finals.

The 2000 NBA Finals were a huge moment for Kobe Bryant, but things didn't go smoothly at first. In Game Two against the Indiana Pacers, Kobe got injured when he landed awkwardly on another player's foot. He sprained his ankle badly and had to sit out for the rest of the game. It was a scary moment because Kobe was such an important part of the team. He even had to miss Game Three to recover, which was tough for him because he loved to be in the middle of the action, especially in such an important series.

However, Kobe wasn't the type to stay down for long. By Game Four, he was back on the court, ready to help his team. The game was intense, and things got even more challenging when Shaquille O'Neal, the Lakers' biggest star, got into foul trouble due to aggressive defense and had to sit out. In basketball, getting into "foul trouble" means that a player has committed too many personal fouls during the game. Each time a player commits a foul, they move closer to being disqualified, which typically happens after six fouls in the NBA. In this case, Shaq had been playing physical defense, blocking shots, and contesting plays aggressively, but as he accumulated fouls, he was forced to sit out to avoid fouling out of the game completely.

This meant the Lakers needed someone else to step up, and that's exactly what Kobe did. Even though he was still recovering from his ankle injury, Kobe took control of the game. He scored twenty-two points in the second half and made some unbelievable plays. The game went into overtime, and with Shaq on the bench, it was all on Kobe to lead the team. And he didn't disappoint! He made the winning shot in overtime, securing the Lakers' victory and proving that he could handle the pressure, even when the stakes were high.

Then came Game Six, where the Lakers had the chance to win the championship for the first time since 1988. With Kobe and Shaq working together, the Lakers came out strong and won the game, securing the championship. At just twenty-one years old, Kobe had won his first NBA title, and he had shown everyone that he was not only a star but also a player who could show up when his team needed him the most. It was the start of something special, and Kobe's championship dreams were just beginning!

The following season, 2000–2001, Kobe's game reached a whole new level. He averaged 28.5 points per game, and once again led the team in assists. But off the court, there were some problems brewing between Kobe and Shaq. Both players wanted to be the best, and as Kobe became a bigger star, he didn't want to share the spotlight as much. Despite their differences, Kobe and Shaq worked together when it mattered most, and the Lakers had an incredible run in the playoffs. They won fifteen out of sixteen playoff games, one of the best performances in NBA history. In the NBA Finals, they defeated the Philadelphia 76ers to win their second straight championship. Kobe was unstoppable in the playoffs, averaging 29.4 points, 7.3 rebounds, and 6.1 assists per game, and Shaq even called him the best player in the league.

By the 2001–2002 season, Kobe had fully established himself as one of the top players in the NBA. He played in eighty games that season, a career high, and set a new personal record when he scored fifty-six points in a game against the Memphis Grizzlies. He was named All-Star MVP for the first time after a fantastic performance in Philadelphia, even though some fans booed him because the Lakers had beaten their team in the Finals the year before. But Kobe didn't let it bother him; instead, he thrived under the pressure.

In the playoffs, the Lakers faced a tough challenge in the Western Conference Finals against the Sacramento Kings. The series went all the way to seven games, but Kobe and the Lakers pulled through, advancing to their third straight NBA Finals. In the Finals, the Lakers faced the New Jersey Nets, and Kobe was once again spectacular. He averaged 26.8 points, 5.8 rebounds, and 5.3 assists per game. At only twenty-three years old, Kobe became the youngest player ever to win three championships in a row. His ability to take over games, especially in the fourth quarter, earned him a reputation as a clutch player, someone who could be counted on when the game was on the line. A clutch player is known for performing well under pressure, often making crucial shots or plays during critical moments, particularly in the final minutes of close games. They thrive in high-stakes situations where the outcome depends on their performance, demonstrating composure and effectiveness when others might falter.

While Kobe was becoming a superstar on the basketball court, his personal life was also changing. In 2000, when Kobe was twenty-one, he met Vanessa Laine, who was seventeen at the time and working as a background dancer on a music video. The two started dating and fell in love quickly. By May 2000, they were engaged, and a year later, on April 18, 2001, they got married. Their wedding took place at a church in California, and although it was a happy moment for Kobe and Vanessa, not everyone was on board. Kobe's parents didn't attend the wedding because they were unsure about the relationship. Despite that, Kobe and Vanessa were happy together and focused on building their life as a married couple.

Kobe's early 2000s were a dream come true. He had won three straight NBA championships with Shaq, established himself as one of the best players in the world, and started a new chapter in his personal life by getting married. But even though he and Shaq were an incredible duo on the court, things weren't always perfect. Kobe was growing more confident in his own abilities and wanted to be seen as the leader of the team. Even so, their teamwork brought the Lakers three championships in a row, making them one of the most powerful duos in NBA history. As Kobe continued to rise in the basketball world, both his career and personal life were moving fast, setting the stage for even more challenges and successes.

FIVE

Challenges and Growth: Life Beyond the Court

In the 2002–2003 NBA season, Kobe Bryant was already a superstar, but he was about to face new challenges and grow both on and off the court. That season started strong for Kobe, showing everyone just how much he had improved over the years. In the very first game, he put up an impressive performance with twenty-seven points, ten rebounds, five assists, and four steals. Even though the

Lakers lost to the San Antonio Spurs, it was clear that Kobe was ready for another incredible season.

Not long after, on November 1, Kobe had one of his best games of the season. He recorded a triple-double, which means he had double-digit numbers in three different categories: thirty-three points, fifteen rebounds, and twelve assists. That game helped the Lakers secure a win against the LA Clippers, and it showed how versatile Kobe was — he wasn't just a scorer, but someone who could help his team in many different ways.

But basketball wasn't the only thing happening in Kobe's life. In January 2003, something even more important and life-changing happened — Kobe became a father for the first time. His wife, Vanessa, gave birth to their daughter, Natalia Diamante Bryant. Kobe was overjoyed to welcome his baby girl into the world. Becoming a dad brought a new sense of responsibility and focus to Kobe's life. He was no longer just a basketball player; he was also a father, and that made him even more determined to be the best he could be, both on and off the court.

Kobe loved his daughter deeply, and while basketball was still a huge part of his life, Natalia gave him a new perspective. He now had someone to play for, someone to inspire, and someone to set an example for. This new chapter as a father fueled Kobe's drive to keep pushing himself to new heights in his career.

Kobe's incredible season continued on January 7, 2003, when he set an NBA record for the most three-pointers made in a single game. A three-pointer is a long-distance shot from beyond the three-point line, and Kobe made twelve of them in one game against the Seattle SuperSonics. This amazing performance left fans and other players in awe of his shooting skills. By the end of that season, Kobe was scoring an impressive average of thirty points per game, and he even went on a historic streak, scoring forty or more points in nine games in a row. In February of that year, Kobe averaged 40.6 points per game, making it feel like no one could stop him.

But Kobe wasn't just about scoring. He also set personal bests that season, grabbing 6.9 rebounds, making 5.9 assists, and getting 2.2 steals per game. This showed that Kobe was more than just a scorer — he was one of the most complete, or well-rounded, players in the league. He was honored by being named to both the All-NBA First Team (meaning he was one of the five best players in the league) and the All-Defensive First Team (one of the best defenders in the league). Although Kobe came in third in the voting for the Most Valuable Player (MVP) award, it was clear that he was one of the top players in the NBA.

Unfortunately, despite Kobe's incredible individual performance, the Lakers didn't have the same success as a team. They finished the regular season with a 50–32 record and were knocked out of the playoffs in the Western

Conference semifinals by the San Antonio Spurs, who would go on to win the championship. It was a disappointing end to a great season, but Kobe was determined to come back stronger.

Before the next season, the Lakers made some big moves, adding NBA All-Stars Karl Malone and Gary Payton to their team. The team was ready to make another push for the championship, but Kobe faced one of the biggest challenges of his life off the court. In the summer of 2003, he was arrested for sexual assault. This became a major event in Kobe's life and caused him to miss several games as he had to attend court hearings. Sometimes, he would go to court during the day and then fly to play games later that night. The pressure was intense. Every time Kobe stepped on the court, the media followed, and the crowd's reactions were mixed. Some fans still supported him, while others were more critical. It was an incredibly difficult time for Kobe, as he had to balance his legal battles with his basketball career.

Even with everything happening off the court, Kobe kept playing at a very high level. One of the most exciting moments that season happened in the final game of the regular season when the Lakers were playing against the Portland Trail Blazers. The Lakers needed to win this game to take the Pacific Division title, and Kobe stepped up in a big way. He didn't just make one big shot — he made two buzzer-beaters to win the game! A buzzer-beater is when a player makes a shot just before the clock runs out.

With Kobe, Shaquille O'Neal, Karl Malone, and Gary Payton, the Lakers made it all the way to the 2004 NBA Finals. Everyone thought the Lakers would win easily, but they were defeated by the Detroit Pistons, who won the championship in just five games. Kobe averaged 22.6 points per game in the Finals, but his shooting wasn't as good as usual, and the Lakers struggled to get past the Pistons' strong defense.

After that loss, things started to change for the Lakers. Phil Jackson, the head coach, didn't have his contract renewed, meaning he wouldn't be coaching the team anymore. Then, Shaquille O'Neal was traded to the Miami Heat, marking the end of a major era for the Lakers. This was a big turning point for the team and for Kobe, as he would now take on an even bigger role.

That summer, Kobe had the chance to leave the Lakers and join another team, the LA Clippers, who offered him a six-year, $100 million contract. But in the end, Kobe decided to stay with the Lakers, signing a seven-year deal worth $136.4 million. He was committed to the team, even though Shaq was no longer there, and he was ready to lead the Lakers into a new chapter.

The 2004–2005 season was a tough one for Kobe. Without Shaq and Phil Jackson, the Lakers struggled. Kobe's reputation had also taken a hit due to the events of the past year. People were talking about him differently, and some even questioned if he could lead a team by himself. One of the hardest blows came when Phil Jackson released a book called *The Last Season: A Team in Search of Its Soul*. In the book, Jackson was critical of Kobe, calling him "uncoachable." This created even more tension and made things difficult for Kobe as he tried to prove himself as the leader of the team.

Midway through the season, the Lakers faced another challenge when their coach, Rudy Tomjanovich, resigned due to health issues. Without a strong head coach, the Lakers struggled even more. Kobe did everything he could to carry the team, averaging 27.6 points per game, the second-highest in the league (the highest scorer that season was Michael Jordan, who led the NBA with an impressive 29.6 points per game), but the Lakers finished the season with a 34–48 record, missing the playoffs for the first time in over a decade. It was a tough season for Kobe, who also had public disagreements with other players, including Karl Malone and Ray Allen.

The conflict with Karl Malone stemmed from an incident in 2004 when Malone allegedly made inappropriate comments toward Kobe's wife, Vanessa, during a Lakers game. Kobe confronted Malone, and their relationship, once close, was never the same afterward.

Kobe's disagreement with Ray Allen was more basketball-related. In a 2004 interview, Allen criticized Kobe's playing style, suggesting that Kobe was overly focused on personal success rather than teamwork. Allen predicted that Kobe would struggle once Shaquille O'Neal left the Lakers. This public critique sparked tension between the two players.

Although it was a difficult time, these years were a period of growth for Kobe. He learned how to deal with criticism, pressure, and personal struggles, all while continuing to work hard and push himself to be the best. He stayed focused on improving his game and didn't let the tough moments define him. This phase of his life was about learning and growing, both as a player and as a person, and it set the stage for Kobe to come back stronger in the years to come.

SIX

Redemption: Winning Without Shaq

After Shaquille O'Neal left the Lakers in 2004, Kobe Bryant found himself at a critical point in his career. Many people questioned if he could lead the Lakers to another championship without Shaq by his side. For Kobe, this was a chance to prove that he could succeed on his own and strengthen his place as one of the greatest players in basketball history.

The 2005–2006 season was a turning point for Kobe. After a difficult period, the Lakers brought back Phil Jackson as head coach, the same coach who had helped Kobe and Shaq win three championships together. Despite some past disagreements, Kobe was happy to see Phil return, and together, they worked well to rebuild the team. Kobe knew that with Phil's coaching and his own determination, the Lakers had a real chance to make it back to the top.

That season became one of the most remarkable in Kobe's career, especially when it came to scoring. On December 20, 2005, Kobe had a legendary game against the Dallas Mavericks, where he scored an incredible sixty-two points in just three quarters. He didn't even need to play in the fourth quarter because the Lakers were already dominating, leading 95–61. Kobe's scoring performance alone had surpassed the entire Mavericks team by the end of the third quarter, 62–61, making it unnecessary for him to return to the court. Given the massive lead and the game being effectively decided, the Lakers chose to rest Kobe for the final quarter. This feat was extraordinary, as no player had ever outscored an entire team through three quarters since the NBA introduced the shot clock. Fans were left in awe, realizing Kobe was performing on a whole new level.

Another important moment came on January 16, 2006, when the Lakers faced the Miami Heat, the team Shaq had joined after leaving the Lakers. There had been tension between Kobe and Shaq ever since their split, but before this game, the two superstars surprised everyone by shaking hands and even hugging. It was a sign that the fight between them was finally cooling down, and they were able to put their differences aside.

However, the most iconic moment of Kobe's season came just days later. On January 22, 2006, in a game against the Toronto Raptors, Kobe did something that will be remembered forever in NBA history. He scored eighty-one points, the second-highest total in a single game ever, behind only Wilt Chamberlain's 100-point game in 1962. What made Kobe's eighty-one-point game so special was that the Lakers were actually losing at halftime, but Kobe's amazing performance helped them come back and win the game 122–104. He made tough shots from everywhere on the court, driving to the basket, shooting from the outside, and creating his own scoring opportunities. By the time the game was over, Kobe had scored sixty-six percent of his team's points, an incredible feat that left everyone in awe.

Kobe didn't stop there. Throughout January 2006, he kept scoring at a record pace, averaging 43.4 points per game for the entire month, the eighth-highest in NBA history. He also became the first player since 1964 to score forty-five points or more in four consecutive games. By the end of the season, Kobe had set a new record for the Lakers by scoring an average of forty or more points in twenty games, which was the most any Lakers player had ever done in a single season. He also broke another record by scoring a total of 2,832 points during that season, which was the highest number of points scored by any player in a single season in Lakers history. This showed just how amazing Kobe was at scoring and how important he was to his team.

He ended the year as the league's top scorer, averaging 35.4 points per game, making him just the fifth player in NBA history to average at least thirty-five points per game in a season. Although Kobe finished fourth in the Most Valuable Player (MVP) voting, he received twenty-two first-place votes, showing how much respect he had earned from the league.

Later in the season, Kobe made a big change by announcing that he would switch his jersey number from eight to twenty-four starting in the next season. Twenty-four was the number Kobe had worn during his early high school days, and he wanted a fresh start as he moved into the next phase of his career.

The Lakers made it to the playoffs, and in the first round, they faced the Phoenix Suns, who were one of the best teams in the league. Kobe played amazingly well, and the Lakers were able to win three of the first four games, giving them a 3–1 series lead (meaning they only needed one more win to move to the next round). In Game Four, with the game almost over, Kobe made an important shot that tied the game and sent it into overtime. Then, in overtime, Kobe made another shot to win the game for the Lakers. It seemed like the Lakers were about to beat one of the strongest teams in the league and move forward in the playoffs.

However, the Suns fought back, and the Lakers couldn't win the series. In Game Six, despite Kobe scoring fifty points, the Lakers lost in overtime. The series went to a deciding Game Seven, and in that game, the Lakers struggled. Kobe was criticized for only taking three shots in the second half, and the Lakers were eliminated by the Suns. It was a tough way to end the season, but Kobe's individual performances throughout the year showed everyone that he was still one of the best players in the league.

The same year in 2006, Kobe's second daughter, Gianna Maria-Onore, also lovingly called Gigi, was born, adding a great deal of joy to Kobe's personal life! Kobe was overjoyed with her birth and loved being a father and spending time with his daughter, even in the middle of his challenging professional life. Despite his busy NBA schedule, Kobe made it a priority to be present for his family. He often spoke about how he would fly home immediately after games to make it back in time for school drop-offs, bedtime stories, or to attend his daughters' activities.

As the 2006–2007 season began, Kobe's switch to jersey number twenty-four represented a new chapter in his career. He continued to be a dominant player, making his ninth All-Star appearance and winning the All-Star MVP trophy for the second time, after scoring thirty points in the game. But the season wasn't without its challenges. Kobe was involved in a few incidents on the court that led to suspensions, including one where he accidentally hit San Antonio Spurs' guard Manu Ginóbili with his elbow while trying to make a shot. The league reviewed the play and suspended Kobe for the next game, saying his arm movement was unnatural. Later in the season, a similar incident occurred, and Kobe was suspended again.

Despite these setbacks, Kobe remained focused on helping the Lakers succeed. On March 16, 2007, he had another incredible performance, scoring sixty-five points in a game against the Portland Trail Blazers. That game ended the Lakers' seven-game losing streak, and Kobe followed it up by scoring fifty points in the next game against the Minnesota Timberwolves. He didn't stop there — Kobe went on to score sixty points in the next game against the Memphis Grizzlies, becoming the second player in Lakers history to score fifty or more points in three straight games. The only other Laker to do that was Elgin Baylor in 1962.

Kobe wasn't done yet. In the very next game, he scored fifty points again, this time against the New Orleans/Oklahoma City Hornets. This made Kobe only the second player in NBA history, after Wilt Chamberlain, to score fifty or more points in four consecutive games.

Although the Lakers made it to the playoffs, they were once again eliminated by the Phoenix Suns in the first round. Despite the early exit, Kobe won his second straight scoring title, and his jersey became the top-selling NBA jersey in both the United States and China, showing just how popular he was around the world.

Kobe's 2005–2007 journey was one of redemption. After the departure of Shaq and a few tough seasons, Kobe proved to everyone that he could still be a dominant force in the NBA. He had shown that he could lead the Lakers and be successful on his own, setting records, winning scoring titles, and giving fans unforgettable moments along the way.

SEVEN

The Mamba Mentality: Defining Greatness

Kobe Bryant's legendary career wasn't just about his physical skills; it was shaped by something more powerful — his mindset, known as the Mamba Mentality. This mentality was all about hard work, determination, and pushing through obstacles, no matter how difficult. Kobe called himself the "Black Mamba," inspired by the snake known for its speed, precision, and deadly strike. Just like the snake, Kobe wanted to be fast, focused, and unstoppable. He adopted the Mamba Mentality to stay sharp, overcome challenges, and rise to the top. It's what defined Kobe as one of the greatest basketball players of all time and helped him achieve incredible success both on and off the court.

In 2007, Kobe was at a point in his career where he wanted more for the Lakers. On May 27, 2007, it was reported that Kobe had asked Jerry West, the former Lakers General Manager who originally brought Kobe to the Lakers, to return to the team. Kobe wanted the team to improve, and he felt West could help make that happen. While he denied saying he wanted to be traded if West didn't return, Kobe did later express frustration with the team, especially after a rumor spread that Kobe was responsible for Shaquille O'Neal's departure from the Lakers.

That season, Kobe continued to dominate on the court. On December 23, 2007, he became the youngest player in NBA history to score 20,000 points at just twenty-nine years old, breaking another milestone in his incredible career. Although this record was later broken by LeBron James, it showed how consistent and brilliant Kobe had been over the years. He also had some amazing individual games that season, including one on March 28, 2008, where he scored fifty-three points and grabbed ten rebounds in a tough loss to the Memphis Grizzlies.

But as great as Kobe was, he also faced challenges. In February 2008, Kobe injured the small finger on his shooting hand during a game. It was a serious injury, tearing a ligament and even causing a small fracture. Doctors recommended surgery, but Kobe decided to play through the pain instead of missing the rest of the season. He said he wanted to delay surgery so he could help his team and play in the upcoming Olympic Games. This decision showed Kobe's toughness and commitment to his team.

That season, the Lakers made an important trade and added Pau Gasol, an All-Star player known for his exceptional skills and versatility, and who would help Kobe lead the team. With Gasol's help, the Lakers ended the regular season with fifty-seven wins and twenty-five losses, which was the best record in the Western Conference. This meant the Lakers were one of the strongest teams going into the playoffs. Kobe's leadership and outstanding play earned him his first MVP award on May 6, 2008. It was a proud moment for Kobe, who had worked so hard to earn that honor. Even Jerry West was there to celebrate with him, marking how far Kobe had come since he was first drafted by the Lakers.

Kobe didn't just stop with the MVP award. He led the Lakers through the playoffs, where they swept the Denver Nuggets in the first round and won a tough series against the Utah Jazz and San Antonio Spurs. This took the Lakers to the 2008 NBA Finals, where they faced their longtime rivals, the Boston Celtics. Although Kobe played well, the Lakers lost in six games, marking a heartbreaking end to the season. But Kobe didn't give up. The defeat against the Celtics fueled him to come back stronger the next year.

In the 2008–2009 season, Kobe and the Lakers were determined to win. They started the season by winning their first seven games and tied a franchise record by starting the season with a 17–2 record. Kobe was again selected to the All-Star Game, his eleventh consecutive appearance, and he kept racking up amazing performances, including a game on February 2, 2009, where he scored sixty-one points against the New York Knicks at Madison Square Garden. This was a record for the most points ever scored in that famous arena, and it showed once again how unstoppable Kobe could be.

Kobe's success continued into the 2009 NBA All-Star Game, where he was named co-MVP alongside his former teammate Shaquille O'Neal. The two players had shared many great moments together, and even though they had their differences, this honor showed that they could still shine together, even as rivals.

By the end of the regular season, the Lakers had the best record in the Western Conference with sixty-five wins. Kobe was once again selected to the All-NBA First Team and the All-Defensive First Team, proving that he wasn't just an incredible scorer but also one of the best defenders in the league.

In the 2009 playoffs, Kobe and the Lakers were on a mission. They defeated the Utah Jazz in five games, then took on the Houston Rockets in a grueling seven-game series. After that, they faced the Denver Nuggets in the Western Conference Finals, where Kobe's leadership helped the Lakers win the series in six games, sending them back to the NBA Finals for the second straight year.

In the 2009 NBA Finals, the Lakers faced the Orlando Magic, and Kobe was determined not to let this chance slip away. He played some of the best basketball of his career, averaging 32.4 points, 7.4 assists, 5.6 rebounds, and 1.4 steals per game. His outstanding performance earned him his first NBA Finals MVP trophy as the Lakers won the championship in just five games. This was a huge moment for Kobe because it was his fourth championship but the first one he had won without Shaq.

Kobe's performance in the Finals was compared to Michael Jordan and Jerry West, two of the greatest players in NBA history. Kobe became the first player since Jordan to average at least thirty points, five rebounds, and five assists in a Finals series for a title-winning team. His ability to dominate both offensively and defensively made it clear that Kobe wasn't just great — he was one of the best to ever play the game.

Kobe's journey wasn't just about the championships and the records. It was about the Mamba Mentality — the idea that greatness comes from pushing yourself to be better every single day. It's about never giving up, no matter how tough things get. Whether Kobe was dealing with injuries, losing in the Finals, or facing criticism, he always came back stronger. His dedication to the game, his incredible work ethic, and his mental toughness are what made him a legend.

Kobe's Mamba Mentality didn't just inspire basketball players; it inspired people everywhere to work hard, stay focused, and never give up on their dreams. He proved that with the right mindset, anything is possible, and that's what truly defined Kobe Bryant's greatness.

EIGHT

Final Championship Run: The 2009 and 2010 Titles

The 2009–2010 NBA season was a special one for Kobe Bryant and the Los Angeles Lakers. After winning the championship in 2009, Kobe and his team were determined to defend their title and win another one. This season was filled with dramatic moments, tough challenges, and incredible victories, as the Lakers pushed themselves toward another championship.

Early in the season, Kobe continued to show why he was one of the most clutch players in basketball. Kobe proved this time and again, making six game-winning shots during the season. One of the most memorable moments came on December 4, 2009, when the Lakers faced the Miami Heat. With just seconds left on the clock, Kobe hit an unbelievable one-legged, buzzer-beating three-pointer over Dwyane Wade, giving the Lakers a 108–107 victory. Kobe later said it was one of the luckiest shots he had ever made, but it added to his legend of being a player who could deliver when it mattered most.

Just a week after that amazing shot, Kobe suffered an avulsion fracture in his right index finger during a game against the Minnesota Timberwolves. This kind of injury happens when a small piece of bone is torn away by a tendon or ligament, and it can be very painful. Despite this, Kobe chose to keep playing through the injury instead of taking time off to heal. His toughness and dedication to the game were on full display. In fact, just five days later,

Kobe hit another game-winning shot, this time in overtime against the Milwaukee Bucks.

Kobe's season was filled with impressive milestones as well. On January 21, 2010, Kobe became the youngest player in NBA history to reach 25,000 career points, breaking Wilt Chamberlain's record. It was yet another reminder of Kobe's consistency and greatness over his career. Shortly after, Kobe surpassed Jerry West to become the all-time leading scorer in Lakers franchise history, a huge accomplishment considering the many great players who had played for the team.

However, Kobe's season wasn't without challenges. In addition to his finger injury, he also dealt with an ankle injury that forced him to miss five games. He even had to sit out the 2010 NBA All-Star Game, despite being the leading vote-getter. But, as always, Kobe came back strong. He returned to the court and hit another clutch shot, a three-pointer that gave the Lakers a one-point lead with just four seconds left in a game against the Memphis Grizzlies.

Throughout the season, Kobe continued to amaze fans with his game-winning shots. One of the most memorable came on March 9, 2010, when Kobe made his sixth game-winner of the season in a victory against the Toronto Raptors. It was clear that, even with injuries, Kobe was still the player the Lakers turned to when they needed someone to win the game.

As the regular season came to a close, Kobe signed a three-year contract extension worth $87 million on April 2, 2010. This ensured that he would remain with the Lakers for the next few years, continuing to lead the team. Despite missing some games due to injuries, the Lakers finished the season with the best record in the Western Conference and were ready for another playoff run.

In the playoffs, the Lakers faced the Oklahoma City Thunder in the first round. Led by young stars like Kevin Durant, the Thunder put up a tough fight, but the Lakers defeated them in six games to advance to the next round. The Lakers then faced the Utah Jazz and swept them in four games, moving on to the Western Conference Finals.

In the Western Conference Finals, the Lakers played against the Phoenix Suns. Kobe had an incredible series, including a standout performance in Game Two, where he had thirteen assists, setting a new playoff career high for himself. The Lakers won the series in six games, securing their spot in the NBA Finals for the third straight year.

The 2010 NBA Finals were a rematch of the 2008 Finals, where the Lakers had lost to their biggest rivals, the Boston Celtics. This time, Kobe and the Lakers were determined to come out on top. The series was intense, and it came down to Game Seven in Los Angeles. In that final game, the Lakers fell behind by thirteen points in the third quarter, but they didn't give up. Kobe, despite struggling with his shooting, led the comeback. He scored ten of his twenty-three points in the fourth quarter and grabbed fifteen rebounds, tying an NBA Finals record for the most rebounds by a shooting guard.

In the end, the Lakers won Game Seven with a score of 83–79, defeating the Celtics and winning the 2010 NBA Championship. This victory was Kobe's fifth championship, and he was named the NBA Finals MVP for the second straight year. After the game, Kobe said this was the most satisfying championship of his career, especially because it was against the Celtics, the Lakers' long-time rivals.

With this win, Kobe had proven that he could lead the Lakers to championships without Shaquille O'Neal, something that had been a big question for years. Kobe had shown that his Mamba Mentality — his drive to always be the best — had paid off, and he was now firmly established as one of the greatest players in basketball history.

Even after winning five championships, Kobe wasn't done. He wanted to win a sixth title to match his idol, Michael Jordan, and he remained as determined as ever to keep competing at the highest level. The Lakers started the 2010–2011 season by winning their first eight games, and Kobe continued to break records. On November 11, 2010, in a game against the Denver Nuggets, Kobe became the youngest player to reach 26,000 career points at thirty-two years of age.

The following year, during the 2011 NBA All-Star Game, Kobe won his fourth All-Star MVP award, breaking the record for the most All-Star MVPs in NBA history. He continued to climb the all-time scoring list, finishing the season in sixth place with more than 27,000 career points.

The 2009–2010 NBA season solidified Kobe Bryant's legacy as one of the game's greatest, as he led the Lakers to their second consecutive championship. His clutch performances, resilience through injuries, and leadership in crucial moments — particularly in Game Seven of the Finals against the Celtics — proved his ability to lead without Shaquille O'Neal.

NINE

Injuries and Setbacks: The Battle to Keep Going

As Kobe Bryant's career progressed, he faced many challenges — especially from injuries. These setbacks tested his resilience, but his mentality kept him pushing forward, no matter how tough things got.

In 2011, Kobe received a special treatment called Orthokine therapy in Germany to help with the pain in his left knee and ankle. This therapy involved injecting his own blood platelets into the injured areas to help them heal. Even with this treatment, Kobe's body was starting to feel the effects of years of intense play. That season, Mike Brown replaced Phil Jackson as the Lakers' head coach, and Kobe started the season with an injured wrist. But, in true Kobe fashion, he didn't let the injury slow him down.

On January 10, 2012, Kobe had an amazing game against the Phoenix Suns, scoring forty-eight points. Kobe even joked afterward, "Not bad for the seventh-best player in the league," referring to a preseason ranking that had placed him below other top players. He didn't stop there. Kobe went on to score above forty points in his next three games, proving that he was still one of the best in the game. It was the sixth time in his career that he scored forty or more points in four straight games, a feat only surpassed by the legendary Wilt Chamberlain.

Later that year, during the 2012 NBA All-Star Game, Kobe achieved another big milestone. He passed Michael Jordan to become the all-time leading scorer in All-Star Game history, scoring twenty-seven points in that game.

However, things didn't go smoothly for Kobe in that game. During the third quarter, Kobe was fouled hard by Dwyane Wade, and as a result, he suffered a broken nose and a concussion. A concussion is a type of head injury that can make a person feel dizzy or confused, and continuing to play with one can be dangerous. Despite these painful injuries, Kobe didn't stop playing. He stayed on the court, proving once again how tough and determined he was. Kobe always pushed through, even when others might have sat out to recover.

Later in the season, in April, Kobe bruised his left shin and this injury caused him to miss seven games. A bruise like this can be painful and make it hard to run or jump. But as soon as he felt strong enough, Kobe returned just in time to help the Lakers finish the regular season and get ready for the playoffs. Once again, Kobe showed that nothing could keep him away from the game he loved.

During the playoffs that year, Kobe and the Lakers faced tough competition. After winning the first round, they moved on to play the Oklahoma City Thunder, a team with some of the league's rising stars, including Kevin Durant. The Thunder were a strong team, and even though Kobe played hard and gave everything he had, it wasn't enough to beat them. The Lakers lost the series in the second round, which means they were eliminated from the playoffs and couldn't move forward to compete for the championship.

This loss was especially tough because it marked Kobe's final appearance in the postseason — the part of the season when teams compete for the NBA Championship. Although he had led the Lakers to many victories in the past, this time, Kobe's efforts couldn't bring another title to Los Angeles. Even though they didn't win, Kobe showed his usual fight and determination, but sometimes, even the best players face obstacles they can't overcome.

The 2012–2013 season brought hope for the Lakers as they acquired two star players — Dwight Howard and Steve Nash — to join Kobe on the team. But things didn't go as planned. The Lakers started the season poorly, losing their first three games for the first time in thirty-four years. Coach Mike Brown was fired, and Mike D'Antoni took over. D'Antoni had known Kobe since his childhood, as both had lived in Italy when Kobe's dad was playing there and D'Antoni was also a basketball star.

Despite the rough start, Kobe kept pushing himself and hit another major milestone on December 5, 2012, when he became the youngest player in NBA history to score 30,000 points at just thirty-four years and 104 days old. He joined a group of legends like Wilt Chamberlain, Michael Jordan, Kareem Abdul-Jabbar, and Karl Malone as one of the only five players to ever reach that milestone.

Kobe continued to perform at a high level, even though the season was filled with challenges. On March 30, 2013, Kobe surpassed Chamberlain to become the fourth-leading scorer in NBA history. But as the season went on, the Lakers struggled, and Kobe started playing almost forty-eight minutes per game to keep the team in the playoffs. An NBA game consists of forty-eight minutes, divided into four twelve-minute quarters, meaning Kobe was playing the entire game without rest. Prior to this, he typically played around thirty-five to thirty-eight minutes per game, which is already a heavy load. Playing nearly the full game meant he was shouldering an enormous physical and mental burden.

On April 10, 2013, Kobe delivered one of the greatest performances of his career, scoring forty-seven points, grabbing eight rebounds, and making five assists, four blocks, and three steals in a single game. No other player in NBA history had ever posted those stats in one game. Just two days later, Kobe's season took a heartbreaking turn.

In a game against the Golden State Warriors on April 12, 2013, Kobe felt a sharp pain in his leg. He had torn his Achilles tendon, a tough band of tissue at the back of the ankle that helps with walking and running. It's one of the worst injuries a basketball player can face. This injury would end his season and keep him off the court for months. Kobe was devastated, knowing that the Lakers' chances of making the playoffs would be much harder without him. But even after the injury, Kobe walked back onto the court to take his free throws before being helped off, showing just how determined he was.

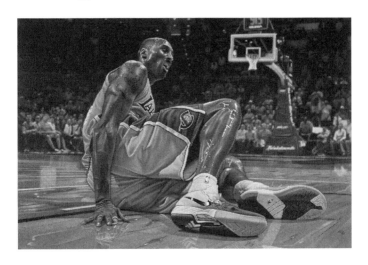

Kobe had surgery the next day, and doctors said it would take six to nine months for him to fully recover. He had averaged 27.3 points, 5.6 rebounds, and six assists per game before the injury, proving that he was still one of the best players in the league. The Lakers made the playoffs, but without Kobe, they were swept by the San Antonio Spurs in the first round.

After months of rehab, Kobe returned to practice in November 2013, but the 2013–2014 season had already started. He signed a two-year contract extension worth $48.5 million, making him the highest-paid player in the league. However, just six games into his comeback, Kobe suffered another setback — a fracture in his left knee that would sideline him for the rest of the season. Even though he had been voted into the NBA All-Star Game, Kobe didn't feel he deserved it and chose not to play. The Lakers finished the season with one of the worst records in the team's history.

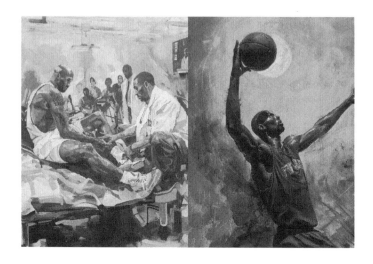

Kobe returned for the 2014–2015 season, his nineteenth season with the Lakers. Though he was getting older, Kobe continued to show flashes of his greatness. On November 30, 2014, in a game against the Toronto Raptors, Kobe recorded his twentieth career triple-double, with thirty-one points, twelve assists, and eleven rebounds. At thirty-six years old, he became the oldest player in NBA history to achieve those stats in a single game.

Just a few weeks later, on December 14, 2014, Kobe passed Michael Jordan to become the third all-time leading scorer in NBA history, adding yet another achievement to his already legendary career. But the season took a turn when, in January 2015, Kobe tore his rotator cuff in his right shoulder. Incredibly, he kept playing in the game, shooting, passing, and dribbling with his left hand. The injury would require surgery, and Kobe's season was once again cut short.

Through the countless injuries and the difficult rehab sessions, Kobe's family was always by his side. Vanessa, his wife, was a constant source of strength, encouraging him to keep going, even when the pain seemed unbearable. His daughters were his inspiration — reminding him of why he worked so hard. "Whenever I felt like giving up," Kobe said in an interview, "I thought about my daughters and how I wanted them to see me as someone who never quit, no matter the challenge." Their presence kept him grounded, and knowing he had their support gave him the motivation to push through every injury and setback.

So, even though Kobe's injuries were piling up, his love for his family and his Mamba Mentality kept him fighting. Even when his body couldn't keep up with his spirit, Kobe never gave up. Through all the injuries and setbacks, he remained dedicated to his team, his fans, and his legacy. Kobe's battles against injuries showed everyone what it meant to be truly determined and never give up, no matter how tough things got.

TEN

The Farewell Tour: Kobe's Final Season

Kobe Bryant's final season, the 2015–2016 NBA season, was a special one, filled with moments of celebration, reflection, and a bittersweet farewell to the game he loved. After playing twenty seasons with the Los Angeles Lakers, more than any player had ever spent with one team, Kobe announced that this would be his last season. It marked the end of an incredible career, but it wasn't an easy season for him. Injuries, challenges, and the aging of his body made this final chapter tough, but Kobe faced it all with the same determination that had defined his entire career.

At the start of the 2015–2016 season, Kobe suffered a calf injury that caused him to miss the last two weeks of the preseason games. However, being the fighter he was, he returned to play in the Lakers' season opener, setting a new NBA record for playing twenty seasons with the same team, breaking John Stockton's record of nineteen seasons with the Utah Jazz.

But as the season progressed, it became clear that Kobe was no longer the unstoppable player he once was. On November 24, 2015, the Lakers played the Golden State Warriors, and Kobe had one of the worst games of his career, scoring only four points in twenty-five minutes and hitting just one of his fourteen shots. It was a tough moment for Kobe, but it was also a sign that his body wasn't able to keep up the same way it used to.

A week later, on November 29, 2015, Kobe made a huge announcement. In a heartfelt letter published on *The Players' Tribune*, Kobe revealed that he would retire at the end of the season. In his letter titled "Dear Basketball," Kobe wrote about how he had fallen in love with the game at just six years old. He described the deep connection he felt with basketball but acknowledged that his body was telling him it was time to let go. Kobe wrote, "My heart can take the pounding. My mind can handle the grind. But my body knows it's time to say goodbye." It was a touching message that showed just how much the game meant to him and how hard it was for him to let go.

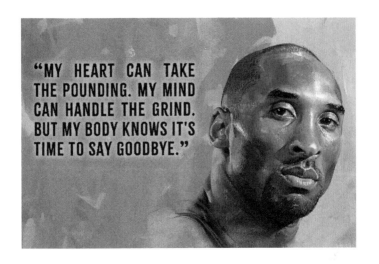

"MY HEART CAN TAKE THE POUNDING. MY MIND CAN HANDLE THE GRIND. BUT MY BODY KNOWS IT'S TIME TO SAY GOODBYE."

As Kobe embarked on his farewell tour during his final NBA season, his family was never far from his thoughts. The decision to retire had been made easier by the knowledge that he would be able to spend more time with Vanessa and their daughters. While he was sad to say goodbye to the game that had shaped his life, Kobe was excited to embrace the next chapter as a full-time husband and father. His family traveled with him during the farewell tour, sharing in the celebrations and milestones. Seeing his daughters in the stands and hearing their cheers reminded Kobe that his legacy wasn't just about basketball, but also about the love and support of his family.

In his final NBA season even though Kobe wasn't playing as well as he used to, he still gave his best effort. He was taking about seventeen shots per game, which was the most on his team, but he was only making about thirty-one percent of them, which was the lowest shooting percentage of his career. Kobe's style of play had changed — he now used more pump fakes (a trick to get defenders to jump) and took more long-range shots. However, his three-point shooting had dropped to just nineteen percent, the lowest in the league. Even with these struggles, Kobe kept playing hard, showing his determination and love for the game, even though his skills weren't what they used to be.

Throughout the season, Kobe requested that opposing teams not make a big deal about his retirement with on-court ceremonies or gifts. He didn't want the attention to be focused on him, preferring the challenge of boos over cheers. But despite his wishes, teams around the league couldn't help but honor him. Even in cities where Kobe was often booed, like Boston and Philadelphia, he received standing ovations and tributes. Fans recognized that they were witnessing the end of a legendary career, and the respect for Kobe grew, even in places where he had once been seen as the enemy.

One of the most exciting moments of the season came on February 3, 2016, when Kobe scored a season-high thirty-eight points in a win over the Minnesota Timberwolves. He made seven three-pointers and scored fourteen of the Lakers' final eighteen points in the last five minutes of the game, helping to end the team's ten-game losing streak. At thirty-seven years old, Kobe became just the fourth player in NBA history over the age of thirty-seven to score at least thirty-five points, five rebounds, and five assists in a single game. It was one of those magical Kobe moments, reminding fans just how special he was, even in the final stretch of his career.

Kobe was also selected as the leading vote-getter for the 2016 NBA All-Star Game, receiving one-point-nine million votes, ahead of superstars like Stephen Curry. This All-Star Game was special because it would be Kobe's last, and the fans wanted to see him one more time on the biggest stage. During the game, his Western Conference teammates offered to feed him the ball to help him win another All-Star MVP award, but Kobe declined. He wasn't looking for individual awards — he just wanted to enjoy the moment and soak in the love from the fans.

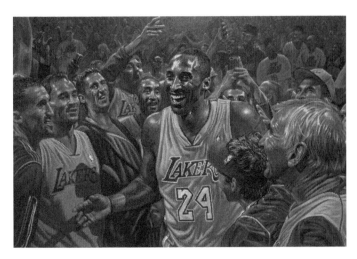

But the biggest moment of Kobe's farewell season came on April 13, 2016, when he played his final NBA game. The Lakers faced the Utah Jazz, and Kobe, at thirty-seven years old, gave the performance of a lifetime. In front of a packed crowd at Staples Center, Kobe scored an unbelievable sixty points, leading the Lakers to a 101–96 victory. Even more amazing, he outscored the entire Jazz team in the fourth quarter, with twenty-three points to their twenty-one. The entire arena was buzzing with excitement as fans cheered on every shot he made.

Kobe's sixty-point performance was the highest score in the NBA that season, and he became the oldest player in NBA history to score sixty or more points in a game. As the final seconds ticked away, Kobe stood on the court, surrounded by teammates, fans, and his family, soaking in the moment. It was the perfect ending to an incredible career. After the game, Kobe said, "What can I say? Mamba out," signaling the end of his legendary journey.

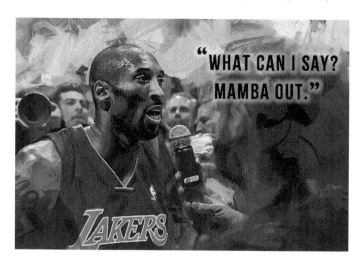

The Lakers finished the season with a 17–65 record, the worst in franchise history, but that didn't matter on this night. Kobe had given the fans one last unforgettable performance, reminding everyone why he was one of the greatest to ever play the game.

Kobe's final season wasn't about wins or championships —
it was about celebrating a career that had inspired millions
of people around the world. It was a farewell to the game
he had given his heart and soul to for twenty years.
Through injuries, setbacks, and challenges, Kobe never
gave up, and his final season was a testament to his
determination, his passion, and his Mamba Mentality. It
was a season that basketball fans would never forget, as
they said goodbye to one of the game's all-time greats.

ELEVEN

Family Life: Kobe's Heart and Soul

Kobe Bryant's life wasn't just defined by basketball — his family was the true center of his world. After every game and practice, Kobe would return to the people who mattered most to him: his wife Vanessa and their four daughters. While his achievements on the court were legendary, it was his role as a husband and father that he cherished most deeply.

Kobe met Vanessa Laine in 1999 when she was just seventeen and working as a background dancer in a music video. Despite Kobe's rising fame, he was immediately captivated by Vanessa's beauty and kindness, and the two started dating soon after. Their relationship moved quickly, and they became engaged only six months later, eventually marrying on April 18, 2001. Kobe was just twenty-two years old at the time, and Vanessa was eighteen.

Vanessa Bryant, who is of Mexican descent, largely stayed out of the spotlight throughout Kobe's career, choosing to focus on their family. Though she didn't pursue a public career, Vanessa has always been active in charitable work, particularly through the Kobe and Vanessa Bryant Foundation, which supports families in need, education, and the encouragement of young athletes. In recent years, Vanessa has taken on a more visible role, particularly after Kobe's passing, becoming a prominent advocate for women's sports and continuing their shared work through the Mamba & Mambacita Sports Foundation. This foundation, renamed in honor of Kobe and their daughter Gianna, helps underserved athletes and young women pursue their athletic dreams. Vanessa's strength and resilience have become an inspiration to many, as she continues to preserve Kobe's legacy while raising their daughters.

Kobe and Vanessa's family grew to include four daughters, each of whom held a special place in Kobe's heart. Their oldest daughter, Natalia Diamante Bryant, was born in January 2003. Known for her bright personality and academic excellence, Natalia shares her father's drive and determination. Though she was once a skilled volleyball player, Natalia decided to focus on her education after Kobe's passing. She enrolled at the University of Southern California (USC) in 2021, where she has pursued her studies with the same dedication Kobe showed on the court. Natalia has also stepped into the world of modeling, signing with IMG Models and balancing her academic and professional life.

Kobe and Vanessa's second daughter, Gianna Maria-Onore Bryant, was born in May 2006 and was affectionately called "Gigi" by her family. Gigi was not only Kobe's daughter but also his basketball prodigy. From a young age, she displayed an incredible passion for the game, much like her father. Kobe often said that Gigi was determined to carry on his basketball legacy and had dreams of playing in the WNBA. Kobe and Gigi shared an unbreakable bond through basketball, with Kobe coaching her team, the Mamba Lady Mavericks, and attending her games as her biggest supporter. Gigi's talent and ambition left a lasting impression on the basketball world.

The Bryants' third daughter, Bianka Bella Bryant, was born in December 2016. Known for her bright smile and playful nature, Bianka quickly became the joy of the Bryant household. Kobe often shared glimpses of his time with Bianka on social media, showing their playful moments together. Though she was still young when Kobe passed, Bianka carries on the legacy of love and joy that her father embodied.

Their youngest daughter, Capri Kobe Bryant, was born in June 2019. Capri, lovingly called "Koko" by her family, was just seven months old when Kobe and Gigi passed away. While she will grow up without knowing her father personally, Vanessa and the rest of the Bryant family work hard to keep Kobe's memory alive for her, ensuring that she understands the incredible legacy her father left behind.

Although Kobe was very close to his parents growing up, as his career and personal life evolved, their relationship became strained. The tension between them escalated in 2013 when his parents attempted to auction off some of his personal things without his consent. This caused a public rift, leading to a period of estrangement. Despite these difficulties, Kobe expressed in interviews his hope that they would eventually reconcile.

Though Kobe's relationship with his parents remained complex, his bond with his sisters endured throughout his life. His sisters, Sharia and Shaya, stayed out of the spotlight but were supportive of their brother and his family, maintaining close connections with Kobe's daughters.

Outside of basketball and family life, Kobe and Vanessa shared a deep love for travel. The Bryants frequently explored new destinations as a family, from exotic vacations to simple getaways. Kobe often said that traveling allowed him to spend quality time with his family, especially during the off-season, when they could relax and create lasting memories together.

Moreover, Kobe's interests outside of sports were as diverse as his talents. He was an avid reader and writer, spending hours studying not only basketball strategies but also the worlds of business, storytelling, and creativity. Some of his favorite books included *The Alchemist* by Paulo Coelho, which he often credited with helping him during challenging times, and *Relentless* by Tim Grover, a book that aligned with Kobe's intense work ethic and "Mamba Mentality." His curiosity led him to launch his own entertainment company, Granity Studios, where he produced films, wrote books, and developed content to inspire future generations.

The Bryant family also had a few beloved pets over the years, including dogs that were often seen in family photos and videos. Kobe was known to have a soft spot for animals, and his daughters, especially Gigi and Natalia, shared his affection for their furry companions. Over the years, they had several beloved dogs, including Crucio, a black Labrador Retriever, who was a constant companion to the family for over ten years. Sadly, Crucio passed away in early 2022. The family frequently shared moments with Crucio, and Kobe himself was close to the dog, even posting videos of Crucio playing in their pool back in 2013.

After Crucio's passing, the family welcomed a new member, Loki, a black German Shepherd, into their lives. Vanessa Bryant introduced Loki to the world via Instagram, where she shared pictures of the dog with their daughters, noting how happy he made the family. Loki quickly became an important part of the Bryant household, filling the void left by Crucio. These pets not only brought joy to the Bryants but also helped the family cope during difficult times, adding warmth and comfort to their lives.

Kobe's role as a father wasn't just about showing up for games or big events — he was deeply involved in the day-to-day activities of his daughters. Whether it was driving them to school, attending dance recitals, or helping with homework, Kobe prioritized his family above all else. He often spoke about how being present for his daughters' milestones was the most important thing in his life. He embraced fatherhood with the same intensity and dedication that he brought to basketball, making sure that his daughters knew they were always his top priority.

The Bryants' family life was filled with love, laughter, and an unbreakable bond. Kobe's legacy lives on not just through his basketball accomplishments, but through the family he cherished and the values he instilled in them. Even after his passing, Vanessa and their daughters continue to honor Kobe's memory by staying close, supporting each other, and carrying forward the lessons of hard work, resilience, and love that he left behind.

TWELVE

Legacy Beyond Basketball: The Icon Lives On

Even after Kobe Bryant retired from basketball, his life remained busy and full of new challenges. He didn't just sit back and relax; he continued working hard, just like he always had on the basketball court. One of the biggest things Kobe did after leaving the NBA was starting his own entertainment production company called *Granity Studios*. Through this company, Kobe was able to bring his creative ideas to life, and one of his biggest accomplishments was writing and producing an animated short film called *Dear Basketball*. The film was based on a letter he wrote about his love for the game and his journey through basketball. In 2018, the film won an Academy Award (an Oscar) for Best Animated Short Film, making Kobe the first professional athlete to win an Oscar.

But Kobe didn't stop there. He was also passionate about helping young athletes and inspiring kids to dream big. He created a fantasy book series called *The Wizenard Series*. The series is set in the world of sports, but it mixes magic and adventure, giving young readers exciting stories to enjoy. The books reflected Kobe's desire to teach young people about hard work, teamwork, and pushing through challenges, but in a fun and imaginative way.

Kobe also opened the Mamba Sports Academy, a special training center for young athletes who wanted to improve their skills in basketball and other sports. The academy was a place where young players could come to work hard, just like Kobe always did, and learn from the best coaches and trainers.

However, the best part of Kobe's retirement was the time he got to spend with his family. By January 2020, Kobe and his wife, Vanessa, had four daughters: Natalia, who was seventeen; Gianna, who was thirteen; Bianka, who was three; and baby Capri, who was only seven months old. Kobe loved being a dad and cherished every moment he had with his girls. He often said that his second daughter, Gianna (whom he called Gigi), was the most like him. Gigi shared Kobe's love for basketball and was a fierce competitor. She dreamed of playing college basketball and later starring in the Women's National Basketball Association (WNBA). Kobe was incredibly proud of her and even coached Gigi's basketball team, the Mamba Lady Mavericks, which was part of his Mamba Sports Academy.

On January 26, 2020, Kobe, Gianna, and several other members of the Mamba Lady Mavericks team were on their way to a basketball game, flying from Orange County to the Mamba Sports Academy in Thousand Oaks,

California, where Gianna was set to play. They were traveling by helicopter, something Kobe often did during his NBA career to save time. That morning, the sky was very foggy, and about forty minutes into the flight, the pilot lost control. The helicopter crashed into the side of a mountain. Kobe, Gigi, and everyone else on board, including two of Gigi's teammates, died in the crash.

The news of Kobe's death shocked the world. People everywhere were heartbroken, and many of his fans, friends, and former teammates couldn't believe that Kobe and Gigi were gone. Shaquille O'Neal, Kobe's longtime teammate and once-rival, cried when he heard the news. By that time, Shaq and Kobe had made peace and become friends again. LeBron James, who was now playing for the Los Angeles Lakers, was also devastated and wept for Kobe. Just the day before Kobe's death, LeBron had passed Kobe on the NBA's all-time leading scoring list. Kobe had congratulated LeBron with a call, telling him, "Keep moving the game forward. Much respect, my brother." It was a reminder of how much Kobe respected the game and those who played it at a high level.

The night after Kobe died, thousands of people gathered outside the Staples Center — the home of the Lakers — to light candles, share memories, and mourn the loss of Kobe, Gigi, and their friends. Buildings across Los Angeles were lit up in purple and yellow, the Lakers' colors, in honor of Kobe.

When Kobe played his last game at Staples Center, he thought he had many more years ahead to achieve new things off the court. "The challenge is to retire and be great at something else," Kobe once said. "There's such a life ahead." Even though his life was cut short, Kobe had already achieved so much beyond basketball.

On February 24, 2020, more than twenty thousand people attended a special memorial service for Kobe and Gigi at the Staples Center. The date — 2/24 — was chosen to honor both Gigi's jersey number, two, and Kobe's jersey number, twenty-four. At the service, Kobe's wife Vanessa gave an emotional speech, talking about how much she loved both her husband and daughter. She called Kobe the "MVP of girl dads" because of how dedicated he was to his daughters. Famous performers like Beyoncé and Alicia Keys also honored Kobe and Gigi with their music, and Shaquille O'Neal gave a heartfelt speech, remembering his time with Kobe.

Even Michael Jordan, one of Kobe's biggest heroes, spoke at the memorial. Jordan said, "In the game of basketball, in life, as a parent, Kobe left nothing in the tank. Kobe gave every last ounce of himself to whatever he was doing." He called Kobe his "little brother" and wished him peace. It was a touching tribute from one of the greatest basketball players ever to another.

Seven months after Kobe's passing, he was inducted into the Naismith Memorial Basketball Hall of Fame, a place that honors the best players in basketball history. It was a fitting recognition of Kobe's incredible career and the hard work he put into everything he did. Kobe's legacy as one of the greatest and most dedicated players of all time will live on forever, not just because of what he did on the basketball court, but because of how he inspired people off the court too.

Kobe Bryant may be gone, but the impact he made on the world of sports, on young athletes, and on fans around the globe will never be forgotten.

Conclusion

Kobe Bryant's journey from Philadelphia to Los Angeles was nothing short of remarkable. He started as a young boy who loved basketball, dreaming of one day playing in the NBA like his father. That dream came true, and Kobe didn't just become an NBA player — he became one of the greatest of all time.

From his early years at Lower Merion High School to the bright lights of the Staples Center, Kobe's career was filled with moments of triumph, challenges, and growth. His work ethic and determination, famously known as the "Mamba Mentality," set him apart from other players. Kobe's ability to push through pain, overcome setbacks, and constantly strive to be the best made him a legend not only in basketball but in life.

He won five championships with the Los Angeles Lakers, earned countless awards, and broke numerous records, but it was his fierce competitive spirit and his love for the game that made him truly unforgettable. Even after retiring, Kobe didn't slow down. He continued to inspire others through his creative work, like his Oscar-winning film *Dear*

Basketball, his *Wizenard* book series, and his Mamba Sports Academy, which helped young athletes chase their dreams.

Kobe was also an incredible father, especially to his daughters, passing on his wisdom and love for basketball to them. His second daughter, Gianna, shared his passion for the sport, and Kobe was proud to coach her and her team, the Mamba Lady Mavericks. Together, they dreamed of great things, and although their lives were tragically cut short, their legacy continues to inspire people everywhere.

Kobe's impact went far beyond basketball. He taught us the importance of hard work, dedication, and believing in yourself, even when the odds are against you. His Mamba Mentality wasn't just about sports — it was a way of life, a mindset that anyone can use to achieve their goals and overcome obstacles.

As Kobe once said, "The most important thing is to try and inspire people so that they can be great at whatever they want to do." And that's exactly what he did. Kobe inspired millions of people around the world, young and old, to pursue their passions and never give up, no matter how tough the journey might be.

Kobe Bryant may no longer be with us, but his legacy lives on in the hearts of those he touched. From his incredible basketball career to his life as a father and mentor, Kobe showed us what it means to live with passion and purpose. His story will continue to inspire generations to come, reminding us that greatness is achieved not just by talent, but by relentless hard work, perseverance, and the courage to follow our dreams.

Mamba out — but never forgotten.

Fun Facts About Kobe Bryant

1. Early Start with NBA Tapes: Kobe began studying NBA tapes at just three years old. Growing up with a professional basketball player as a father, it wasn't long before Kobe developed a deep love for the game and started learning from the best.

2. Friendship with Michael Jackson: Kobe and pop legend Michael Jackson were close friends. They became friends when Kobe was only eighteen. Michael even gave Kobe advice on how to handle fame and develop his work ethic.

3. A Philanthropic Heart: Kobe wasn't just a star on the court; he was also dedicated to helping others. He supported numerous charities, including:

• Participating in a 2012 fundraising effort for Stand Up To Cancer that raised over $80 million.

• Supporting the NBA's *NBA Cares* initiative by helping build homes, stock food pantries, and support children's education.

- Working with sick children through the *Make-A-Wish* foundation, granting wishes to many kids battling illnesses.

4. Incredible Work Ethic: Kobe's daily routine was legendary. He would start his workouts as early as 3:30 AM! His dedication to practicing before anyone else earned him respect and contributed to his long-lasting success. His trainer shared stories of finding Kobe drenched in sweat, practicing hard even before 5 AM.

5. AC Milan Fan: Growing up in Italy, Kobe became fluent in Italian and developed a love for soccer. His favorite team was AC Milan, and even after returning to the United States, Kobe kept an AC Milan jersey and scarf in his locker as a reminder of his love for the club.

6. Most Missed Shots in NBA History: While Kobe was known for his incredible scoring, he also holds the NBA record for the most missed shots (14,481). Despite the misses, Kobe's determination and willingness to take risks helped him win five NBA championships and become one of the greatest players in the game.

7. Failed Music Career: Before focusing entirely on basketball, Kobe ventured into the music industry. He released a solo album titled *K.O.B.E.* and appeared in a remix of Destiny's Child's *Say My Name*. However, his music career didn't take off as expected, and the album was ultimately canceled by Sony Entertainment.

8. Net Worth: By the time of his passing, Kobe Bryant had amassed a net worth of $600 million. His wealth came from his successful NBA career, endorsements, and ventures outside of basketball.

9. Kobe Bryant on the big screen: Kobe appeared in a few movies and TV shows over the years. He also voiced himself in an episode of the popular animated series *The Proud Family* and had a cameo in *Modern Family*.

10. Kobe Bryant and Lionel Messi Team Up: In September 2012, Kobe Bryant teamed up with soccer superstar Lionel Messi to shoot a fun commercial for Turkish Airlines. In the ad, Kobe and Messi hilariously compete for the attention of a young boy, showing off their skills in a playful rivalry.

Kobe's Scores Over Time

Season	Games Played	Minutes per Game	Points per Game	Rebounds per Game	Assists per Game
1996-1997	71	15.5	7.6	1.9	1.3
1997-1998	79	26.0	15.4	3.1	2.5
1998-1999	50	37.9	19.9	5.3	3.8
1999-2000	66	38.2	22.5	6.3	4.9
2000-2001	68	40.9	28.5	5.9	5.0
2001-2002	80	38.3	25.2	5.5	5.5
2002-2003	82	41.5	30.0	6.9	5.9
2003-2004	65	37.6	24.0	5.5	5.1
2004-2005	66	40.7	27.6	5.9	6.0
2005-2006	80	41.0	35.4	5.3	4.5
2006-2007	77	40.8	31.6	5.7	5.4
2007-2008	82	38.9	28.3	6.3	5.4
2008-2009	82	36.1	26.8	5.2	4.9
2009-2010	73	38.8	27.0	5.4	5.0
2010-2011	82	33.9	25.3	5.1	4.7
2011-2012	58	38.5	27.9	5.4	4.6
2012-2013	78	38.6	27.3	5.6	6.0
2013-2014	6	29.5	13.8	4.3	6.3
2014-2015	35	34.5	22.3	5.7	5.6
2015-2016	66	28.2	17.6	3.7	2.8

Timeline of Kobe Bryant's Life

1978:

- August 23: Kobe Bean Bryant is born in Philadelphia, Pennsylvania.

1984:

- Kobe's family moves to Italy after his father, Joe "Jellybean" Bryant, continues his professional basketball career overseas.

1991:

- The Bryant family returns to the United States, settling in Philadelphia after seven years in Italy.

1992-1996:

- High School Stardom: Kobe attends Lower Merion High School in Ardmore, Pennsylvania, where he leads the team to a state championship and becomes a highly touted basketball prospect.

1996:

- June: Kobe declares for the NBA Draft straight out of high school.

- July: Drafted thirteenth overall by the Charlotte Hornets and immediately traded to the Los Angeles Lakers.

- November 3: Kobe makes his NBA debut, becoming one of the youngest players in NBA history.

1997:

- February: Wins the Slam Dunk Contest during NBA All-Star Weekend, becoming the youngest player to do so at eighteen years old.

1998:

- February: Kobe becomes the youngest starter in NBA All-Star Game history at nineteen.

2000-2002:

- Championship Three-Peat: Kobe, alongside Shaquille O'Neal and under the coaching of Phil Jackson, leads the Lakers to three consecutive NBA Championships.

2001:

- April 18: Kobe marries Vanessa Laine in a private ceremony.

2003:

- January: Kobe becomes a father for the first time with the birth of his daughter Natalia Diamante Bryant.

2006:

- January 22: Kobe scores eighty-one points in a single game against the Toronto Raptors, the second-highest point total in NBA history.

- May: Gianna Maria-Onore Bryant (Gigi), Kobe's second daughter, is born.

2008:

- May 6: Kobe wins his first NBA MVP award.

- June: Leads the Lakers to the NBA Finals, but they lose to the Boston Celtics.

2009:

- June: Kobe wins his fourth NBA Championship, and first without Shaquille O'Neal, defeating the Orlando Magic in the Finals. He also earns his first NBA Finals MVP award.

2010:

- June: Wins his fifth NBA Championship, defeating the Boston Celtics in seven games. He is named NBA Finals MVP for the second consecutive year.

2011:

- December 5: Kobe becomes the youngest player in NBA history to score 30,000 career points.

2013:

- April 12: Kobe tears his Achilles tendon during a game against the Golden State Warriors. He undergoes surgery and is sidelined for months.

2015:

- November 29: Kobe announces his retirement at the end of the season in a heartfelt letter, "Dear Basketball."

2016:

- April 13: Kobe plays his final NBA game, scoring an incredible sixty points in a win against the Utah Jazz, marking a fitting end to his legendary career.

2018:

- March: Kobe wins an Academy Award for his short film *Dear Basketball*, based on his retirement letter.

2019:

- June: His youngest daughter, Capri Kobe Bryant, is born.

2020:

- January 26: Kobe and his daughter Gianna tragically pass away in a helicopter crash in Calabasas, California, along with seven others.

2020:

- February 24: A public memorial service, "A Celebration of Life for Kobe and Gianna Bryant," is held at the Staples Center.

2021:

- May: Kobe is posthumously inducted into the Naismith Memorial Basketball Hall of Fame, with Vanessa Bryant delivering an emotional speech in his honor.

References

Biography editors. *Kobe Bryant*. Biography (2023). https://www.biography. com/athletes/kobe-bryant. Accessed October 01, 2024.

Britannica editors. *Kobe Bryant*. Britannica (2024). https://www.britannica. com/biography/Kobe-Bryant. Accessed September 28, 2024.

Bryant, Kobe. *The Mamba Mentality: How I Play*. New York. Farrar, Straus and Giroux, 2018.

Curwen, Thomas and Wharton, David. *Kobe Bryant, from the start, was an athlete like no other*. Los Angeles Times (2020). https://www.latimes. com/sports/lakers/story/2020-01-26/lakers-kobe-bryant-obit. Accessed October 02, 2024.

Gagne, Tammy. *Kobe Bryant: Basketball Superstar*. Minnesota. Abdo Publishing, 2020.

Labrecque, Ellen. *Who Was Kobe Bryant?*. New York. Penguin Random House LLC, 2020.

Lazenby, Roland. *Showboat: The Life of Kobe Bryant*. New York. Back Bay Books, 2016.

Wikipedia contributors. *Kobe Bryant*. Wikipedia (2024). https://en. wikipedia.org/wiki/Kobe_Bryant. Accessed September 22, 2024.

BONUS

Check out my other book, *Simone Biles: A Book For Smart Kids*, and discover the incredible journey of one of the greatest gymnasts in history. As a bonus, you'll get the introduction and first chapter right here. Enjoy!

Introduction

Welcome to the inspiring world of Simone Biles, a gymnast who redefined what it means to be great. Simone Biles is not just an athlete; she's a symbol of determination, courage, and resilience. Her journey from a young girl with big dreams in Columbus, Ohio, to becoming one of the greatest gymnasts of all time is nothing short of extraordinary.

In *Simone Biles: A Book For Smart Kids - Soaring Beyond Limits: The Journey of a Gymnast Who Redefined Greatness,* you'll follow Simone's incredible path to glory, from her early days flipping around on a trampoline in her backyard to standing on top of the Olympic podium with gold medals around her neck. You'll learn how she overcame challenges, faced setbacks, and kept pushing herself to achieve more, always with a smile on her face and a heart full of passion.

But this book is about more than just gymnastics. It's about how Simone has inspired kids and adults alike to dream big, believe in themselves, and never give up, no matter what obstacles they face. Whether she's inspiring audiences with her gravity-defying routines or bravely speaking out about the importance of mental health, Simone has shown the world that true strength comes from within.

As you read about Simone's journey, you'll discover the hard work, discipline, and love for the sport that have driven her to the top. But you'll also see how she's used her platform to make a difference, inspiring a generation of young people to fly beyond their own limits and reach for the stars.

Simone Biles was born on March 14, 1997, in Columbus, Ohio. She was the third of four siblings, with an older sister, Ashley, who was two years older than Simone, an older brother, Tevin, who was four years older and a younger sister, Adria. Adria was two years younger than Simone and the baby of the family.

From a young age, Simone's life was marked by uncertainty and change. Her mother, Shanon Biles, faced significant challenges in caring for her children due to personal struggles and financial instability. Shanon, who battled issues related to substance abuse, found it increasingly difficult to provide the stable environment her children needed. Simone's father, Kelvin Clemons, was largely absent from her life. He struggled with his own challenges and was not involved in raising Simone and her siblings. These difficulties meant that Simone and her siblings often found themselves without the stable support system that most children rely on during their early years.

Just imagine how hard it all must have been for little Simone and Adria, without the help of their parents.

As a result of her mother's difficulties, Simone and her siblings were placed in the foster care system when Simone was just three years old. Foster care is a system designed to provide temporary care for children whose parents are unable to look after them, often due to a variety of challenges such as financial instability, health issues, or other personal struggles. While the foster care system aims to provide a safe and nurturing environment, it can also be an incredibly challenging experience, especially for young children who want stability and the comforting presence of their parents.

For Simone, entering foster care meant being separated from her mother and the familiar environment of her home in Columbus, Ohio. At such a young age, she found herself in unfamiliar surroundings, living with people she didn't know and adjusting to rules and routines that were different from what she was used to. The constant shifting from one foster home to another added to the uncertainty and made it difficult for Simone to form loving relationships or feel secure. Each new home brought a different set of caregivers, some of whom did not fully understand the emotional needs of a child who had already experienced so much sadness in her life.

The experience of moving from home to home, sometimes with siblings and sometimes without, was very disturbing. Simone had to adapt quickly to new environments, while dealing with the confusion and sadness that comes from being separated from her mother and the life she once knew. Imagine waking up each day not knowing what the future holds or where you will be living. This uncertainty can be incredibly frightening, and it was exactly what Simone experienced during her early years.

During her time in foster care, Simone was too young to fully understand why she was being moved from one place to another or why she couldn't be with her mother. But these experiences began to shape her character. The need to adapt to new circumstances taught her perseverance, and the lack of control over her situation taught her the importance of making the most of the opportunities that did come her way. She also learned to be flexible, to adapt to new situations quickly, and to find small comforts in the middle of uncertainty. These are traits that would later serve her well as she started gymnastics, a sport that requires not only physical strength but also mental toughness and the ability to perform under pressure.

Simone and her siblings had spent about three years in the foster care system before their story took a positive turn. During that time, they experienced the instability of moving between different homes. However, things changed when their maternal grandparents, Ron and Nellie Biles, learned that their grandchildren were in foster care. Living in Spring, Texas, a suburban area just outside of Houston, Ron and Nellie were determined to provide a stable and loving home for Simone and her siblings. Nellie was a regional nurse who traveled frequently for her job, while Ron was a retired Air Force sergeant who now worked as an air traffic assistant with the Federal Aviation Administration in Houston.

In 2000, they welcomed Simone, Adria, Ashley, and Tevin into their home. For Simone and Adria, the move to Texas marked the beginning of a new chapter in their lives.

Living with their grandparents in Texas, Simone and Adria found the stability they had been missing. Ron and Nellie, whom Simone affectionately calls Grandpa and Grandma, were committed to giving the girls a secure and nurturing environment. They lived in a comfortable house, where there was always enough food on the table, and where Simone and Adria felt safe and loved. The house was filled with warmth and laughter, and the girls quickly bonded with their new older brothers, Ron II and Adam, who were sixteen and fourteen years old at the time.

As Simone and Adria settled into their new life, they began to feel more at ease. The trauma of their early years started to fade as they experienced the love and care of their grandparents. Ron and Nellie were not just providing a home for the girls; they were giving them a family. The stability and support that Simone found in Texas were crucial in helping her develop the confidence and determination that would later define her career as a gymnast.

In 2003, when Simone was six years old and Adria was four, the Biles family decided to make their commitment to the girls permanent by legally adopting them. This was a monumental decision, not just for Ron and Nellie, but for Simone and Adria as well. The adoption process took place on November 7, 2003, a date that would forever be written in the hearts of the Biles family. On this day, a judge formally recognized Ron and Nellie as the legal parents of Simone and Adria, solidifying their place as members of the Biles family.

For Simone and Adria, this adoption was far more than just a legal formality — it was a moment of emotional significance. Up until this point, their lives had been filled with uncertainty, with no clear idea of what the future might hold. Although they had been living with Ron and Nellie for a few years and had grown to love them deeply, the adoption was the final step in making sure that they would never again have to worry about being separated from their family.

For Ron and Nellie, the adoption was the fulfillment of their deep commitment to providing a loving and nurturing environment for their granddaughters. By making the adoption official, they were not only showing their love and dedication to Simone and Adria but also taking on the full responsibility of parenthood once again. They understood the importance of family and were determined to give Simone and Adria the stable, supportive home they deserved.

That evening, after the adoption was finalized, the family gathered at home to celebrate. As they were getting ready for bed, Simone called out, "Good night, Grandma!" But Nellie gently stopped her and said, "You know, girls, we adopted you both today. So I'm your mother now, and he's your father," she said, pointing at Grandpa Ron. The realization that she now had a mom and a dad brought immense joy to Simone. For the first time in her life, she felt like she truly belonged. She had found her forever home.

While Simone and Adria had settled permanently with their grandparents, Ron and Nellie did not adopt Tevin and Ashley, Simone's older siblings. Instead, Tevin and Ashley were adopted by Ron's sister, Harriet, who was their great-aunt. This arrangement allowed Tevin and Ashley to remain together in Ohio, while Simone and Adria stayed with Ron and Nellie in Texas. This decision was made to ensure that all four children could be cared for in stable, loving homes that could meet their individual needs. Although they were separated geographically, the siblings remained connected as part of an extended family that cared deeply for each of them.

This sense of belonging and security became a very important part of Simone's life. It gave her the emotional strength to pursue her dreams and face the challenges that lay ahead. With the love and support of her new parents, Simone began to thrive. The stability of her home life allowed her to focus on her interests and develop her talents. Little did anyone know at the time, but this young girl from Columbus, Ohio, was destined for greatness.

Thanks for being a reader!

If you enjoyed reading *Kobe Bryant: A Book For Smart Kids*, I'd love to hear what you think! Leaving a review on Amazon is like giving the book a high-five — and it helps other readers find it too. Plus, it's super quick! Just scan the QR code to get started.

Thanks for being awesome and sharing your thoughts!

Magic Matthews

Made in United States
Troutdale, OR
12/23/2024

27218010R00071